How to Write a Paragraph

Grades 6–8

Editor
Barbara M. Wally, M.S.

Editorial Project Manager
Ina Massler Levin, M.A.

Editor-in-Chief
Sharon Coan, M.S. Ed.

Cover Artist
Sue Fullam

Art Coordinator
Denice Adorno

Creative Director
Elayne Roberts

Imaging
Ralph Olmedo, Jr.

Product Manager
Phil Garcia

Publisher
Mary D. Smith, M.S. Ed.

Author

Kathleen Christopher Null

Teacher Created Resources, Inc.
6421 Industry Way
Westminster, CA 92683
www.teachercreated.com

ISBN: 978-1-57690-490-9

©1999 Teacher Created Resources, Inc.
Reprinted, 2009
Made in U.S.A.

Table of Contents

Introduction

Knowing how to write a clear and well-organized paragraph will go a long way toward the success of any future writing that students will do. When students realize that longer pieces of writing are written one paragraph at a time, they will feel empowered as capable and effective writers.

This book will enable you to take the essential unit of good writing, the paragraph, and teach it to your students in its many forms.

Getting Started

In the Getting Started section, you will find pages to introduce the basic concepts of paragraph writing. Included are prewriting activities such as brainstorming and getting ideas.

Essential Parts

Next, you will find a section on the essential parts of a paragraph, which includes main ideas, topic sentences, supporting and body sentences, transitions, and conclusions.

Kinds of Paragraphs

This section covers seven different kinds of paragraph writing: narrative, expository, descriptive, comparison, contrast, opinion, and definitive.

Paragraphs in Action

After students have gained competence in developing ideas and understanding the parts and kinds of paragraphs, they will have the opportunity to practice what they have learned so far with the activities in this section. The paragraph starters in this section can be used in many different ways and whenever you wish. They will make good story starters as well.

Getting Your Act Together

In this section, students will combine all they have learned as they are introduced to essay and letter writing, relating each to paragraph writing.

Paragraph Tools

This section contains a paragraph plan and a checklist to enable students to check their own paragraphs.

Time for Some Fun

Finally, it's time for some fun. This section will reward your diligent students while reinforcing what has been learned.

When your students have completed the activities in this book, they will be well on their way to being creative, capable writers with an understanding of that very important writing unit—the paragraph.

What Is a Paragraph?

If you're going to write anything at all, you should first master the art of writing a paragraph. Books, articles, essays, and stories are all made up of many paragraphs. The paragraph is the basic unit of writing. When you know how to write a good paragraph, you will be able to write many different things with the confidence of a good writer. You will be able to organize your ideas and express yourself more clearly. You will even be able to think better!

A *paragraph* is a short piece of writing with a beginning, a middle, and an ending. A good way to think about how to organize a paragraph is to think about how you talk to your friends. For example, one day when Katie was walking on the beach, she saw a whale in the water. At school the next day, she wanted to tell her friends about it, but they were talking. She said, "You won't believe what I saw yesterday! I saw a whale at the beach!" She got their attention and told them about her topic—the whale. You will do the same thing when you write a paragraph.

With everyone listening, Katie told them all the details. She told how the whale's flukes slapped the surface of the water, how the whale dove under the water, how it came up and looked around and blew vapor from its blowhole, and how excited she felt watching all of this.

Then Katie concluded her story, "And then the whale started to swim rapidly out to sea. I was sorry to see it go, but it was so much fun seeing it play for awhile." Here are the basics:

The Beginning

Every paragraph begins with a *topic sentence*. It gets the attention of the reader and tells what the paragraph will be about. If Katie had said, "I took a walk yesterday," it wouldn't have been as specific or as interesting. So make the first sentence, or topic sentence, of each paragraph interesting and specific, but save the details for the sentences that follow.

The Middle

The sentences that follow the topic sentence add more specific details and tell more about the topic. Sometimes these sentences are called *body sentences*. Every sentence in the body of your paragraph needs to be about the topic. If Katie, after saying she saw a whale, said, "I think I'll get my hair cut short," she would be changing the topic and losing her listeners. You don't want to lose or confuse your readers, so make every sentence prove, or support, your topic.

The End

The last sentence of a paragraph is the *concluding*, or *closing*, *sentence*. In this sentence you will remind the reader what the topic is and what it means. If your paragraph will be followed by another paragraph, your concluding sentence needs to have a *transition* into the next paragraph. For instance, if you were writing an essay about hunting dogs, a paragraph about Irish setters might be followed by a paragraph about springer spaniels. You might end the Irish setter paragraph with "And so, the Irish setter is especially useful as a hunting dog, and the spaniels are similar in their abilities." If you were only writing one paragraph, though, you would not do this, because then your readers would be waiting for you to tell them about spaniels.

4

What Can I Write About?

In order to get started, there are two things you will need. You will need lots of ideas, and you will need a way to organize and connect your ideas.

Here are some suggestions for getting ideas:

- Keep an idea notebook. Get a little notebook that you can carry around with you wherever you go. Most professional writers do this, and for good reason. When ideas come to you, and they will when you have a place to record them, write them in your notebook. Also, write lists of subjects you would like to know more about, things you are curious about, things you wonder about, anything you hear about that seems strange or funny or fascinating, your opinions, your feelings, and anything else that interests you.

- Do a lot of reading. Read books, of course, but also read magazines, newspapers, billboards, cereal boxes, shirts, menus, book reviews, letters, etc. You will get many ideas from reading.

- You can also get ideas from movies, music, school, conversations, encyclopedias, dictionaries, relatives, friends, and by simply paying attention to the things around you.

Keep notebooks and files for your ideas, and when you are stuck for a writing topic, you can find one very quickly.

Once you have a topic, you will need to find a way to make it "grow" into a paragraph. Here is one way. It's called clustering. Here is an example of a student's clustering around the topic "bread."

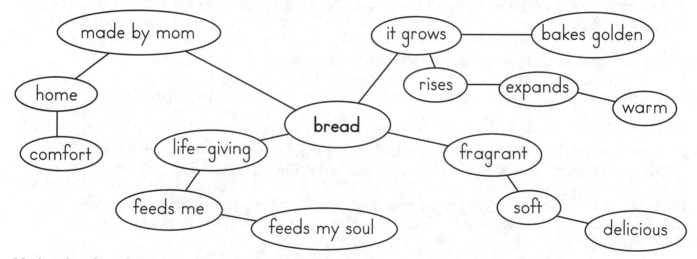

Notice that there is no set pattern for how her clusters grow. Ideas can be connected in any way. Here is the paragraph she wrote after she clustered:

> Bread is my favorite food. Its warm, fragrant welcome brings me home. It is love from my mom as she slices a piece for me. It's soft and delicious and gives me life. I like to see how it grows in the pan and then bakes until golden. Bread is my favorite food. It feeds me while it feeds my soul.

Choose a topic of your own. Write the topic in the center of your page, circle it, and then cluster around it until you have enough details to write about it.

Brainstorm!

Another method for organizing your ideas, and even for getting new ones, is to *brainstorm*. You can brainstorm by yourself, with a friend, with the entire class, with a parent, etc. Brainstorming has rules that need to be followed.

1. Write down every idea that is spoken or thought.

2. Do not judge any ideas. Don't say things like, "That would never work," "What kind of an idea is that?" or "That's silly."

3. Let all the ideas flow. They don't have to make sense, and they don't need to be connected to or related to any other ideas. They just have to be ideas.

4. When you think you have run out of ideas, pause, take a deep breath, and get ready to write some more. There are many pauses in brainstorming, so be sure you really are finished before you stop.

5. When you're sure you have enough ideas and no more are coming, take a look at what you have. Circle those you like the best and look at them again. You will know when you like one idea or combination of ideas the best.

A student wanted to write something about photography, but he wasn't sure what to say. Here is the list he brainstormed with a friend:

camera, lens, light, dark, shadow, flash, black and white, color, fast shutter, fast action, blurred action, stopped action, sports, shooting fast, the right moment, click, motor drive, driving, clicking, film, money, developing, out of focus, try, work hard

After brainstorming, he decided that he wanted to write about being a sports photographer and all the challenges that sports photographers must overcome in order to get good shots.

Brainstorm for a topic. After you choose your topic, cluster or brainstorm again to decide what you want to say about your topic. After you have clustered or brainstormed and feel like you are ready to write, write a paragraph about your topic, including all the specific details.

Extension: Brainstorm with the class on a topic. Write all the ideas on the board. Then have each student write a paragraph from the brainstormed list. When finished, compare paragraphs. In what ways are the paragraphs similar, and in what ways are they different?

Have students take the paragraph they wrote and make it into a story or an essay with three or four paragraphs.

You'll Need These

Once you have good ideas and a topic, you're ready to write a paragraph. Your paragraph will need the following parts:

A Beginning

The first sentence of a paragraph is the *topic sentence*. It tells what the paragraph will be about. Every topic sentence needs a specific subject and a specific feeling or attitude. Read the following example.

> It's really important to me to have hair.

Hair is the subject; *really important to me* is the feeling or attitude.

A Middle

The sentences that follow the topic sentence are called the *body sentences* or *supporting sentences*. They tell more about the topic by adding more details. Each detail in the body sentences should make the topic more interesting or help explain what you mean. Each of these sentences also needs to be about the topic sentence and should support it. Here are some body sentences to support the topic sentence above.

> Sure, we can get along without it—my Uncle Barry is proof of this (he just slaps some sunscreen on his bare skull and he's all set)—but I would still prefer to have hair for many reasons. First of all, I think I would look pretty silly without hair; I have seen myself in a bathing cap. Second of all, I like to play with my hair when I'm bored. I can braid it, twist it, tie it in a bow under my chin, or check for split ends. I also like that it goes wherever I go.

An Ending

The last sentence of your paragraph is the *closing* or *concluding sentence*. In this sentence, you need to remind the reader of what the topic is about and what it means. This is a way for you to tie it all together. Here is a good closing sentence for the paragraph above:

> To me, it's just really important to have hair, and I wonder what Uncle Barry does when he gets bored.

Here is a paragraph that begins with a topic sentence and one body sentence. Finish the paragraph by adding between two and six more body sentences and a concluding sentence. Be prepared to share your paragraph in class.

> I'd really like it if the only thing to drink in the world were chocolate milk. First of all, it is my favorite thing to drink, so I would be happy about that.

_____

_____

Extension: Share the finished paragraphs in class. Did everyone say the same things? Did anyone have something unusual to say? Did anyone who hates or is allergic to chocolate milk have to write a paragraph? Was his or her paragraph as convincing as the others?

Got Any Wise Ideas?

Each of your paragraphs should tell the reader about just one idea. If you have more than one idea, you will need to omit some of them or write more paragraphs. Each of the boxes below contains a set of ideas for a paragraph. Your job is to create a topic sentence that tells what the paragraph will be about and write it on the line at the top of each box. The first one has been completed as an example.

1. **Dessert is the best part of dinner.**

   Chocolate cake is so yummy. Ice cream is always a great dessert. I really like cookies, too.

2. _____

   Participating in sports helps us to be healthy. We learn teamwork when we play sports. Sports can also help our brains to work better.

3. _____

   Rubber cars would just bounce off of each other. Metal cars crush, and people get hurt. Rubber cars would not need to be waxed.

4. _____

   It tastes good. It has tomato sauce, cheese, and bread, and those are good for us. We can put lots of vegetables on it, too.

5. _____

   They have rollercoasters, and those are fun. Vendors sell things like cotton candy and churros there. It has brightly colored lights and happy music.

6. _____

   I would be able to call and ask a question about my homework. I could answer the telephone when my friends call. I could call 911 if there were an emergency.

7. _____

   We would not be able to eat and would need others to feed us. We would not be able to brush our hair or our teeth. If we had no elbows, we would not be able to talk on the telephone.

8. _____

   They are affectionate animals. They can be trained to help people. They can help protect families.

For Younger Students: Provide the following list of topic sentences to match with the idea boxes:

- We should all participate in a sport.
- Cars should be made of rubber instead of metal.
- Pizza is the perfect food.
- I want to go to an amusement park this weekend.
- I should have my own telephone.
- We would be in big trouble without elbows.
- Dogs make good pets.

So What's the Point?

Each sentence in a paragraph must relate to the main idea stated in the topic sentence. In the paragraphs below, cross out each sentence that is not related to the topic.

1. When I grow up, I want to be an architect. Architects get to design buildings, and I would love to do that. I have a sketch pad full of my design ideas. My sister wants to be a teacher. I don't think that would be as much fun. My mom says that after I graduate from architecture school, I can design a house for her. I would love to do that and to design lots of other buildings, too.

2. Snowboarding is one of the best sports a person can do. Skiing is also good to do. A snowboarder gets into really good shape. Snowboarding is also very creative because there are lots of ways to move on a snowboard. Skateboarding is another way to stay in shape when there is no snow. Snowboarding is a good way to stay in shape, stay healthy, and be creative.

3. To do well in school, one should study every night. If there isn't much homework, there is time to go back over notes or review a chapter. Test taking is easy once you figure out the secrets. It's a good idea to keep up with the classes each night; then, if there is a quiz, one can be ready. Some teachers like to surprise students with a quiz, and some let students know when to study. Each day, teachers add more material, and it's not good to get behind. It only takes a little time, and it is worth it to study each night.

4. Every student should go out for a sport. For one thing, students will make more friends if they participate in a sport. Professional athletes make lots of money. Students who participate in sports are healthier and more fit. A manufacturer may sponsor those who get really good at a sport. They have found that students who participate in a sport do better in school, too. There are many good reasons why every student should go out for a sport in school.

5. My parents are really strange people. There are many strange people in the world. First of all, they go square dancing in these strange, goofy costumes every Saturday. I'm not sure whether there are more strange adults or more strange teenagers in the world. Another thing is they wear funny shorts and hats when they are working in the yard. And they also cry at the weirdest times, like when my class is doing a singing program. And so you see, the strangest people in the world happen to be my parents.

So What's the Point? *(cont.)*

Outlines are good tools for organizing your writing whether you are writing a paragraph, a story, or an essay. To write an outline, you begin with your topic and then divide it into parts. Under each part, you list details. An outline uses either words or sentences for its topic, parts, and details. Outlines do a good job of keeping you focused on the point you want to make.

Here is a sample outline with four subtopics:

School Clothes

   I. Boys' clothing

      A. pants

      B. shirts

         1. T-shirts

         2. polo shirts

  II. Girls' clothing

      A. pants

      B. skirts

      C. shirts

 III. Footwear

      A. shoes

      B. boots

 IV. Outerwear

      A. sweaters

      B. jackets

      C. coats

Choose four or more of the topics below (or choose your own topics) and write a topic outline for each, using four or more subtopics for each outline.

fast food	families	art	soft drinks
water sports	cars	countries	movies
jobs	footwear	cereals	houses
hair styles	school subjects	teams	pet peeves
snow sports	ice cream	pets	homework
	bands	candy	

My Topic Is . . .

Maybe you have heard a classmate, while standing before the class say, "My topic is . . . it's on . . . um, my topic is on the kitchen table at home. I forgot to bring it to school!" Perhaps you have heard, "My presentation is about . . ." or "My speech is about . . . ." When you hear these words, you listen carefully to learn what else the speaker has to say. An audience wants to know what the speech, presentation, or paragraph will be about. In a paragraph, the topic sentence is usually the first sentence. It's an important sentence because it tells what the paragraph will be about. Here are two topic sentences. Circle the one that sounds more interesting to you.

> This is about vegetables.
> In an ideal world, there would be no need for vegetables.

A good topic sentence not only tells what the topic will be; it also says something more about the topic or expresses a point of view.

Here is a list of topics. Your job is to write an interesting topic sentence that tells what you would like to say about each topic. Be sure to write a topic sentence that will make a reader want to read more. Be creative! The first one has been completed as an example.

1. packages *There is something very mysterious and exciting about a package.*

2. high school _____

3. cars _____

4. sleep _____

5. carrots _____

6. sports _____

7. French fries _____

8. magazines _____

9. families _____

10. movies _____

Challenge: Read the topic sentences aloud in class to show the variety of ideas generated. Make copies of the topic sentences, cut them apart, mix them up, and pass five of them to each student. Have the students write a paragraph for each topic sentence they receive.

For Younger Students: Choose five or eight topics instead of ten. Use the leftover topics to challenge the whole class to a brainstorming session for creative topic sentences. Have the class to a finish at least one paragraph with the ideas generated. Have each student come up with at least five topic sentences.

My Topic Is ... *(cont.)*

Write a topic sentence for each of the paragraphs below.

1. _____

   _____

Students would not be looking around to see what their friends are wearing, and they would be able to concentrate on the teacher. We wouldn't be spending as much time or money on clothes. There would be fewer students making fun of those who do not dress in the latest trend. If we were all dressed the same way, we could get down to the business of learning.

2. _____

   _____

I love them, but it's really embarrassing when they go places with me. They are kind of nerdish, and they are always asking questions. They try to give me a hug or a kiss when everybody is around. They come to school and meet my teachers and tell them things about me. All I can do is be nice and love them and know that one day I'll be just like them with my own kids!

3. _____

   _____

First of all, the locker room is so smelly and hot. Next, we have to change clothes in the middle of the day! Then we have to go outside and sweat while whistles are blasted in our ears. And if that's not enough, I am always late for my next class. I think this is one class I could do without.

Read each paragraph aloud to make sure that your topic sentence works well with all the sentences that follow.

Challenge: Using old magazines or newspapers, cut out paragraphs that are interesting. If you wish, you can enlarge them with a copy machine. Cut the topic sentence from each paragraph. Pass the paragraphs out and challenge students to write new topic sentences for each paragraph.

For Younger Students: List the following possible topic sentences for the paragraphs above on the chalkboard. Allow students to choose from the list, or to use the list for ideas.

- I hate P.E. class!
- We should wear uniforms to school.
- Uniforms are a good idea for students.
- P.E. is not my favorite class.

- My parents are so embarrassing!
- We should do without P.E. class.
- My parents embarrass me all the time!
- I am in favor of school uniforms.

Help!

A topic sentence does not work alone to explain the main idea of a paragraph. It would not be able to do that. It needs some help. The sentences that help are known as body sentences or supporting sentences. They help by making the main idea more clear.

Here are some topic sentences that need help. Create a body sentence to follow each of the topic sentences below:

Lima beans are disgusting! _____

_____

School should be two days per week. _____

_____

Pizza is the best food on the planet. _____

_____

We need our thumbs. _____

_____

Eating is fun. _____

_____

There should be robots to do chores. _____

_____

Everyone needs a pet. _____

_____

We should laugh every day. _____

_____

Candy is not good for us. _____

_____

Extension: Take four of the topics above and write a full paragraph for each, including a closing sentence.

Help! *(cont.)*

These paragraphs are lacking support. Can you help? The three reasons that support the topic sentences are missing. Your job is to create the supporting sentences by filling in the blanks. Be sure to write complete sentences.

1.   There are three reasons why I would not eat an insect even if I were offered a hundred dollars. The first reason is that _____

Another reason is _____

_____

Finally, I would not eat an insect because _____

_____

Please don't ask me to eat an insect!

2.   There are three reasons why I love food. First of all, _____

_____

_____

_____

Now try some more on another piece of paper. Use three or four reasons for each topic. Don't forget a concluding sentence.

- I should have my own room for the rest of my life.
- Turtles make great (horrible) pets.
- I would like to be locked in the mall.
- I would (would not) like to travel by hot air balloon.

Challenge: Write a topic sentence of your own. Mix your sentence with those written by your classmates. Draw a topic sentence and write a paragraph on the topic. Remember to use three or four supporting points.

For Younger Students: Before the assignment, have students complete a paragraph as a class. Discuss the importance of supporting sentences and how they prove one's point.

Everybody Needs Some Body

Every paragraph needs a body. The *body* of a paragraph consists of sentences that tell about the subject. It is in the body of the paragraph that one uses specific details like *who*, *what*, *where*, *when*, *why*, and *how*. Here is a paragraph with the body sentences underlined.

> Michael really likes computers. <u>When he was a little boy, he used computers to play games and draw pictures. When he was a teenager, he used computers to communicate with friends all over the world. Today, Michael has his own computer business on the Internet.</u> It seems like Michael has always been a computer nut.

The Body Snatchers

In these paragraphs the bodies have been snatched. There are only a topic sentence and a closing sentence. Create three or four body sentences for each paragraph.

> I would like to build my own little shack in the backyard. _____
>
> _____
>
> _____
>
> Having a place to call my own would make all the difference in the world.

> The toothbrush is a great invention. _____
>
> _____
>
> _____
>
> And so, the toothbrush, we see, has many uses, but my favorite use is for brushing my teeth.

> Everybody should dance. _____
>
> _____
>
> _____
>
> There are so many good reasons why everybody should dance, why would anyone choose to sit?

Extension: Find some interesting paragraphs in magazines and newspapers. With a highlighter, mark the topic and concluding sentences. Bring three samples to school. In turns, your teacher will call on students to write their topic and concluding sentences on the board. Class members will write body sentences that they think might fit and share them with the class.

Everybody Needs Some Body *(cont.)*

Pretend that you are an English teacher and you gave your students an assignment to write a paragraph about their pets. Here are some of the paragraphs that were turned in to you. You must give each paragraph an "A," a "B," or a "C" grade. You are looking to see whether the students wrote a clear and interesting topic sentence, added good supporting body sentences that stay on the topic, and ended with a concluding sentence that fits. Put the grade in the box at the bottom of each paragraph and write a brief comment about why you gave the grade you did.

1. I love my pet. She is a small foxhound named Friskie. She loves pizza and tortillas better than anything. Once she got lost and got hit by a car, and we couldn't find her for weeks. Finally, Grandpa found her at the pound. She had stitches from being hit by the car. Sometimes she cries when she wants me to come outside and play with her.

Grade: ☐ Comment: _____

2. A pet is an animal that people keep. I have two turtles, a snake, a hamster, a parakeet, and a cat. The turtles' names are Hector and Jane. The snake's name is Indy. The hamster's name is Porky. The parakeet's name is Petey. The cat's name is Sylvester. The turtles like to eat lettuce. The snake likes to eat mealworms and mice. The hamster likes to eat grapes and nuts. The parakeet likes to eat birdseed. And the cat likes to eat my lunch.

Grade: ☐ Comment: _____

3. My cat's name is Snookie, and she likes to sleep at the end of my bed every night and purr me to sleep. In the morning she wakes me up. My best friend Cassandra has a cat, too; her name is Lucky. I think cats make great pets. I love my cat.

Grade: ☐ Comment: _____

4. I have a special pet rabbit named George. George is brown and white and very, very soft. George gets excited when he sees me coming to his cage with some carrots or celery. He stands up on his hind legs and waves his paws at me. George also really likes dandelions. He will hop all over the yard, gobbling the dandelions. At night, he falls asleep in my lap. George is a very special rabbit.

Grade: ☐ Comment: _____

Extension: Now that you've had some experience with grading paragraphs, take a look at some of your own and think about how you would grade them and how you would improve them.

And So?

Chronology means the order in which things happened. When you write or talk about something that happened to you or something that you do, it needs to be in the right time order. The things you write about in a paragraph should usually be in *chronological order* to make sense.

Here is a paragraph that is out of order. Can you make any sense of it? Write the paragraph in chronological order.

> They were out of bagels, so I had to get a jelly donut. I thought I could get a bagel and some orange juice. I thought they were due tomorrow! When I got home, no one was there, and I had forgotten my keys. Then when I tried really hard, it came open and some of it spilled on my pants! I ate while I walked to school. When I went to open the hot chocolate, it wouldn't open. I didn't have time to eat breakfast, so I stopped at the donut store on the way to school. I accidentally set it for 6 P.M. instead of 6 A.M. First of all, my alarm never went off. Then it was really hot and burned my tongue. They were out of orange juice, so I had to get hot chocolate. When I got to history, the teacher asked for our reports. I said, "Don't ask." After school, in track, my pants ripped. Of course, the next thing that happened is the jelly donut spurted and got red stuff down the front of my light blue shirt. I was so embarrassed. I had a very bad day today. When my mom came home, she found me sitting on the front porch. She asked me, "How was your day?"

Extension: Write a paragraph, in chronological order, on one of these topics: what you did after school yesterday, how your day went today or last week, how to make macaroni and cheese, or how to ride a skateboard or bicycle.

And Then?

All of the sentences you write in your paragraphs need to tie together as a unit. They need to flow and be connected as well as make sense. The words and phrases that are used to connect ideas are called *transitions*. Here are some examples of transitions:

first	**next**	**then**	**finally**	**and so**
however	**nevertheless**	**so**	**today**	**suddenly**
and then	**after that**	**in addition**	**at last**	**although**

Here are some paragraphs that lack transitions. Rewrite them with transitional words or phrases. Read your work aloud to see if it flows.

1.   We're going to have an exchange student next month. She needs to send in her papers to the exchange program. She will write us and send her picture. We will write her and send pictures. She will travel to our country, and we will meet her!

2.   It's a good idea to get enough rest each night. Sleeping in too long on the weekends could cause problems. It can confuse our bodies, and then we will have trouble sleeping at night. If we get too much sleep, we waste time and may be too wound up to be able to concentrate. When Monday morning comes, we will be even more tired. It is a good idea to get enough rest. We need to do so in moderation.

3.   I was not able to do my homework last night. My brother broke his arm, and we had to take him to the doctor's office. It was really late when we got home. I set my alarm to get up early to do my homework. I was so tired that I slept through it and had to hurry to get to school!

Extension: Collect transitional phrases. There are many more than those listed on this page. On television and the radio, transitions are called *segues* (seg-ways). Listen to talk shows or news broadcasts on the radio or TV news programs to hear segues between topics. Jot down some of them ("Speaking of unpredictable, here is Johnny Hail with the weather. What kind of unpredictable weather is in store for us this week, Johnny?"). Look for transitional phrases in newspaper and magazine articles and stories. Start a collection with the entire class contributing. Look through them as a creative warmup before your next writing assignment.

And Finally!

The final sentence of your paragraph is the *concluding sentence* or closing sentence. It comes after all the details and explanations have been included in the body sentences of your paragraph. The closing sentence should express the *specific feeling, attitude,* or *point* of the paragraph. It should summarize the paragraph. Look closely at the last sentence of this paragraph, for instance:

A woman would make a good president. Women learn to do many things at once. They can plan a PTA meeting while changing diapers and cleaning house. They can carpool while giving a French quiz and planning after-school activities. With her ability to cope with more than one activity at a time, a woman is especially qualified to be a leader of our country.

Here are some unfinished paragraphs. Complete each one by adding a few more details and a closing sentence. Use the back of this page if you need more room.

Skateboarding should be an Olympic sport. First of all, it takes a lot of skill, and it has evolved into an art form. Skateboarding parks are appearing all over the country, so more and more skaters can hone their skills._____

_____

I would make a fantastic president! First, I know how to say things so that they sound good no matter what, for instance,_____

_____

Next, I am used to bossing people around._____

_____

Many rock stars are excellent musicians. Anyone who has ever taken music lessons can tell whether or not someone knows music. _____

_____

_____

Challenge: Share your completed paragraphs with the class. All of the paragraphs began the same, but how did they end? Were they all different? What were some of the most unusual endings? Were any of the endings similar?

For Younger Students: Before assigning the paragraphs, post them, or similar ones, on the board or the overhead projector. Review the role of each sentence in the paragraph (such as topic sentence, supporting sentences that explain or support the topic sentence, etc.) while brainstorming sentences to add to the paragraphs. Talk about what makes a good concluding sentence. Then have students finish the paragraphs on their own.

So What's the Story?

A *narrative* paragraph is a paragraph that gives the details of an experience or event in story form. The details are included in natural time order, or chronological order. You use narrative form when you tell someone all about your day or recall an experience you had. Fill in the blanks below to write a narrative paragraph:

> The first time I ever (cooked, rode a skateboard, babysat, skied, etc.) was a total disaster.
>
> First,_____
>
> _____
>
> Next,_____
>
> _____
>
> Then,_____
>
> _____
>
> Finally,_____
>
> _____
>
> I had never been more (embarrassed, angry, excited, etc.) in my life!

Extension: Choose three of these topics and write a narrative paragraph for each one, or choose one topic and write three to six narrative paragraphs.

earliest memory	first birthday party	best birthday party
last Christmas or Hanukah	first day of school	what happened yesterday
last vacation	first job	what I did last weekend
my morning routine	the route to school	first plane trip

You Had Better Have a Good Explanation!

Another kind of paragraph is the *expository* paragraph. Expository writing gives facts, explains ideas, or gives directions. Below are some topics for expository paragraphs. Choose four, and on four separate pieces of paper, write one paragraph for each topic that you choose.

- Explain how a camera works.

- Tell how to twirl a baton.

- Explain how to groom a horse.

- Explain how to make a watercolor painting.

- Tell how to sew on a button.

- Give the facts about your favorite sports team.

- Tell how to drive a car.

- Explain why you like your favorite candy.

- Tell how to ride a bike.

- Explain the game of football.

- Give the facts about your favorite movie or TV star.

- Tell how to study for a test.

- Tell how you make dinner.

- Explain how to play your favorite musical instrument.

- Give the facts about your favorite animal.

- Explain how to swim.

Challenge: Create a presentation to give orally to your class. In your presentation, tell the class how to make something or how to do something, or tell your classmates the facts about a topic that interests you. Use visual aids and props to make your presentation more interesting.

For Younger Students: Have each student write one paragraph on the topic of his or her choice. They may choose topics of their own, with your approval, or use the ones from the list.

Can You Describe It?

A *descriptive* paragraph gives a clear picture of a person, place, idea, or thing. A good way to write a very clear descriptive paragraph is to use as many of the five senses (hearing, seeing, smelling, tasting, and touching) as you can. You will need to practice your observational skills to write descriptively. Fill in the following to see how observant you are and to practice writing descriptively.

1. If you rode to school this morning on the bus or in a car, describe the driver. Tell what he or she wore, what he or she looked like, what he or she did, like chewing gum or humming to music. If you walked or rode your bike, describe five things you saw on the way (people, animals, the weather, cars, etc.).

   _____

   _____

   _____

2. Without looking at your teacher, describe how he or she looks today (hair, clothing details like textures or colors, etc.)

   _____

   _____

3. Look at the student nearest you and describe what he or she looks like and his or her clothing (be purely objective in your description).

   _____

   _____

   _____

4. Describe the weather today, including the color of the sky.

   _____

   _____

   _____

5. Using the five senses, describe everything you can observe from where you are seated.

   _____

   _____

   _____

Extension: Go to a location such as an airport, restaurant, library, mall, classroom, doctor's office, or park. Write a description of what you see, hear, smell, feel, and taste. Keep a notebook for your observations.

However...

The ability to *compare and contrast* in your writing will give you strength as a writer. A paragraph can be a *comparison* (how your sister and Minnie Mouse are similar), a *contrast* (how you and your sister are different), or both a *comparison and a contrast* (how you and your sister are similar and how you are also different). When you compare and contrast, think of details that prove your point that two people, things, or ideas are the same or different. Here is an example of a comparison paragraph:

My sister and Minnie Mouse are similar in many ways. First of all, they both tend to wear black, white, and red polka dots. Also, my sister has a high-pitched giggle that reminds me of the sound a mouse makes. My sister also wears shoes that are too big for her. There are many other ways, too, but these are the most obvious ways that she is similar to Minnie Mouse.

Here is a contrast paragraph:

My sister and I are different in several ways. My sister likes to play with dolls inside, and I like to climb trees and kick a ball outside. Next, my sister likes to watch movies about love and romance, and I like to watch movies about adventure and crime. Finally, my sister prefers candy and ice cream for desserts, while I prefer donuts and brownies. It's amazing that we're even in the same family, because we are so different!

Here is a comparison and contrast paragraph:

My sister and I are the same in some ways and different in other ways. While my sister likes to play indoors, and I like to play outdoors, we both like to skate at the skating rink. My sister loves to go to the movies and see a love story, while I prefer an adventure, but we both love comedies and a big tub of popcorn. There isn't any dessert that my sister and I both like, but we both always ask mom what's for dessert. Our differences don't keep us apart, but our similarities help keep us together.

Choose four of the topics below and write a paragraph for each:

1. Compare someone you know to a cartoon character.
2. Compare yourself with a famous person.
3. Compare your feet, hands, hair, or eyes with those of your best friend.
4. Contrast yourself with a relative.
5. Contrast dogs with cats as pets.
6. Contrast the mountains with the beach as vacation choices.
7. Compare and contrast snowboarding and skateboarding.
8. Compare and contrast football and baseball.
9. Compare and contrast the requirements of school with the requirements of work.

Extension: Choose a relative or friend that you admire. Choose three points to make (three things to compare and contrast) and write a five-paragraph essay comparing and contrasting you and this friend or relative. The first paragraph will introduce your topic, the second will compare and contrast one of the three points, the third, another point, and the fourth, the last point. Conclude in the fifth paragraph.

I Can Be Very Convincing

When you write a paragraph to express an opinion or to try to convince the reader that your opinion is correct, you are writing a *persuasive* paragraph. Even if you have never written a persuasive paragraph before, you have at least spoken persuasively. How about the last time you tried to persuade a parent to buy you a certain pair of shoes or to let you see a particular movie? You probably had to think first of some ideas that would be convincing or persuasive enough, and then you probably chose your best, or most convincing, ideas.

Here is an example of a persuasive paragraph:

> Everyone should read fiction every day. Mom was right about bedtime stories. Reading stories or novels at bedtime or as a break during the day is a good idea. For one thing, it is relaxing, like a vacation from work and worry. Another good reason is that reading fiction is like traveling. When we read fiction we get to "travel" to other places and "experience" new things. These new experiences expand our minds and strengthen them. When we finish reading fiction, we can go to sleep or back to work feeling refreshed, renewed, and ready.

Choose four of the topics below (or create your own topics), and write a persuasive paragraph for each one. Use your most convincing details.

- Fast food is a great thing in our modern age.
- Fast food will bring down modern society.
- Rap music is very creative.
- Rap music is annoying.
- There are some good reasons for watching television.
- There are few good reasons for watching television.
- Everyone should know how to swim.
- Swimming is not a necessary skill.
- Newspapers are the best place to get one's news.
- Television is the best place to get one's news.

- Shopping is fun.
- Shopping is tiresome and boring.
- I should have my own CD player in my room.
- I should have my own telephone in my room.
- I shouldn't have to go on vacation with my family each year.
- Families should always take a vacation together each year.
- The Internet is mostly a bad thing.
- The Internet is mostly a good thing.
- Everyone should take math in school.
- I shouldn't have to take math in school.

Extension: With a partner, choose or create two opposing topics. One of you should write in favor of the topic and the other in opposition. Read your paragraphs aloud. Did you convince your partner? Did he or she convince you? Have a debate on your topic.

In My Humble Opinion . . .

In an *opinion* paragraph, you don't need to convince the reader that you are right, but you do need to be clear enough so that the reader understands why you have the opinion. In an opinion paragraph, you have a point to make, and your focus is on what it is that you think or feel about something. Your opinion needs to be supported with your reasons for having such an opinion.

After you complete this form, you will be well on your way to being an expert on writing opinion paragraphs.

In my opinion, homework should (should not) be given. First of all, _____

_____

_____

Second, _____

_____

_____

The most important reason why I think homework should (should not) be given is _____

_____

_____

Therefore,_____

_____

_____

Write an opinion paragraph about a topic on which you have a strong opinion or belief. Your opinion will be your topic sentence. Then support your opinion with strong reasons, saving the most important reason for last. Finally, sum up your opinion in the last sentence. (Some ideas for your opinion paragraph are television, violence, war, pollution, drugs, equal rights, education, global warming, etc.)

Extension: Have the entire class choose one to five topics. The students can write one opinion paragraph for each topic. Collect the topics for a book or bulletin board display. In addition, the collected topics could be used for a graphing activity (numbers of students in favor of and against school uniforms, etc.).

Can You Define It?

A *definitive* paragraph is a paragraph that defines something. When you define things, you help others to understand your writing, your opinion, and the point you wish to make. Use the questions below to help you write your definitions. (**Note:** The 10 questions are to help you think; you do not need to use all ten of them.)

1. What is it?
2. What does it look like?
3. How does it feel?
4. What does it smell like?
5. Does it have a sound?

6. What does it do?
7. How is it used?
8. How does it make me feel?
9. Does it have a purpose?
10. What thing or things is it completely different from or similar to?

Define these items by using your imagination and not a dictionary.

A puppy is _____

_____

_____

An artichoke is _____

_____

_____

A camera is _____

_____

_____

Joy is _____

_____

_____

Extension: Find some unusual words in the dictionary. For each word, create three cards. On one card write the dictionary definition. On the remaining cards, create definitions that might fool your classmates. Have a team of three students present the definitions while classmates vote for which definition they think is correct. The majority vote is the class choice. How often were you able to stump your classmates?

26

Pizza Sauce!

Oh, no! You completed your paragraph assignment, but you set it on top of the pizza by accident. When you grabbed your paper, you found that some of your words were missing. Now you will have to add the missing parts before you turn it in. Circle your opinion on the first line, and get going!

Students *should/should not* have to wear uniforms to school. There are four reasons why I think this.

First, _____

_____

_____

Next, _____

_____

_____

Another reason is that _____

_____

_____

Finally, I think that _____

_____

_____

And that is why I think that _____

_____

_____

Watch Out for the Paper Shredder!

You wrote a how-to paragraph and left it on your mom's desk. You came in to see if she had read it just as she was putting some papers in the paper shredder. Your paper was accidentally mixed in with her junk mail. You quickly grabbed your paragraph, but it was too late! The shredder had already eaten parts of your paragraph. Can you rewrite your paragraph in time to turn it in? You wrote about how to do something that you do very well.

It is very easy to _____, and I will tell you how I do it. First, I

_____

_____

Next, I _____

_____

_____

_____

After that, I _____

_____

_____

_____

Finally, I _____

_____

_____

_____

And now you know that it is easy to _____

_____

_____

I Would Like to Visit . . .

Is there some place that you have always wanted to visit? Imagine that you are entering a contest to win a trip to one of the destinations listed below. To enter, you must write a one-paragraph letter that explains why you want to go there. Include in your letter three reasons why you want to make your visit.

The destinations:

- Bahamas
- Bermuda
- Disneyland
- Disney World
- Germany
- Greece

- Hawaii
- Holland
- Jamaica
- India
- Ireland
- Japan

- Legoland
- London, England
- Los Angeles, CA
- Montreal, Canada
- Rome, Italy
- Scotland

- Seattle, WA
- Paris, France
- Tahiti
- Washington, D.C.
- Melbourne, Australia
- Rio de Janeiro, Brazil

Dear Contest Judges,

I would like to go to _____ because

_____

_____

_____

_____

_____

_____

_____

_____

_____

Sincerely Yours, _____

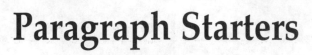

Paragraph Starters

Use these paragraph starters when you need inspiration while practicing paragraph writing. You might want to use some of these ideas for writing an essay (see page 32), a report, or a story.

It would be better if it were light all the time—day and night.	I like to stay up late.
There are many uses for dry beans.	I like to get up early.
Desserts should be eaten first.	Some shoe styles seem really silly.
My brother/sister comes from another planet.	Collecting stamps is an interesting hobby.
It's a good thing that we have thumbs.	There are many uses for a shoebox.
Dogs make the best pets.	I would like to be the governor of my state.
Cats make the best pets.	Sleeping is a very strange thing to do.
We should allow only bicycles on the freeways.	I love to dance.
I would like to live in a space station.	We should never be bored.
Every student in the class should invite the teacher to dinner.	I will never eat squid.
I would like to have lived in the 1800s.	We should be able to go to school in our pajamas.
No one should be allowed to wear red.	I make the best macaroni and cheese.
Anyone can sing.	I love football.

Paragraph Starters *(cont.)*

School starts too early in the morning!	I like llamas.
Everybody should play soccer.	I won't wear anything without a pocket.
I love cookies!	Yellow is the best color for food.
We can eliminate racism.	I love to go to the movies.
I would make a good mom (dad).	Everybody should have a pet.
I can't wait to drive.	This is how to make a great pizza.
I have three favorite bands.	Pollution is a big problem.
Here is my advice about babysitting.	I would like to be a movie star.
My favorite shoes are . . .	If I had three wishes . . .
My favorite subject is . . .	I would like to live in a tree.
I should have my own telephone.	Books will always be popular.
There are lots of reasons why I am glad to be a member of my family.	If I were an animal, I would be a(n) . . .
I would like to be an astronaut.	I like comfortable clothes.

Essay Writing

Now that you can write a paragraph, you can write an essay. An *essay* is made up of several paragraphs and has a structure which, you will be glad to know, is very similar to the structure of a paragraph. Also, just as there are persuasive, explanatory, comparison, contrast, and opinion paragraphs, there are also persuasive, explanatory, comparison, contrast, and opinion essays. Essays can be humorous, personal, or biographical; they can be on any topic you can imagine.

As you gain more and more experience with writing essays, you will experiment with different forms and structures. This form, however, is the one most widely used by novice writers and is a good basic essay structure.

The first paragraph of an essay is the *introductory paragraph*. In the first few sentences, write a broad introduction to your topic. After that, write a bit more specifically about your topic and list the main points (or ideas, arguments, or supports) that you will be using in your essay.

The *body* of your essay is made up of the paragraphs that follow the introductory paragraph. Each of these paragraphs begins with a topic sentence which tells what that paragraph will be about. The sentences that follow the topic sentence give more details, and the last sentence of each paragraph—its closing sentence—provides a bridge or *transition* to the next paragraph.

The final paragraph of your essay is the *conclusion*. In this paragraph you will summarize the points you have made in the body of your essay and come to a conclusion about your topic.

Here is an outline for an essay with three points (arguments, ideas, and supports):

  I. The Introductory Paragraph (*introduces the topic*)

 II. The First Body Paragraph (*explores the first point*)

     A. Topic Sentence

     B. Supporting Ideas

     C. Closing/Transition Sentence

III. The Second Body Paragraph (*explores the second point*)

     A. Topic Sentence

     B. Supporting Ideas

     C. Closing/Transition Sentence

IV. The Third Body Paragraph (*explores the third point*)

     A. Topic Sentence

     B. Supporting Ideas

     C. Closing/Transition Sentence

 V. The Concluding Paragraph (*summarizes the topic and draws a conclusion*)

     A. Topic Sentence

     B. Supporting Ideas

     C. Closing/Transition Sentence

Essay Writing *(cont.)*

And so you see, you already know how to write an essay. An essay is just a group of paragraphs that are all about a single subject. Here is a brief essay to demonstrate. Usually essays are longer than this, with more sentences including specific details in each paragraph.

Introductory paragraph   Artists have always made contributions to society. I would like to do the same. When I grow up, I would like to be an artist. I love art, I enjoy creating art, and I would rather work as an artist than anything else.

First body paragraph   I love looking at art. I love to go to art galleries and see all the art there is. I love to have art around me. I even love the smell of the paints and varnishes. I could be happy just being around art all day long.

Second body paragraph   I enjoy creating art. I like to think about what I see and make sketches. I like to experiment with paints and try different colors. I would be happy to spend all day creating art, if I could.

Third body paragraph   I would rather work as an artist than anything else. I can't even imagine doing any other kind of job. I would be thinking about doing art the whole time I was doing some other job. It's not the easiest job there is, but it's the only job I want to do.

Concluding paragraph   And so, it is clear that more than any other job, I would rather be an artist. I would love everything about it, enjoy the creativity, and even enjoy the hard work of being an artist. I will be an artist when I grow up.

Letter Writing

A letter is like an essay unless it is just one paragraph. Each paragraph of a letter is on one topic. Although letters don't need to follow the same structure as an essay with topic sentences for each paragraph, etc., they would be easier to understand if they were organized that way. When you write a formal or business letter, you will want it to be more structured than you would a casual, friendly letter.

Here is an example of a casual letter. Notice that each paragraph has its own topic.

October 12, 1999

Dear Caleb,

How are you doing? I'm fine. I heard you were sick. Was it the chicken pox? Are you better yet, or are you still scratching?

Did I tell you I got a new pet? It's a boa constrictor. My brother gave it to me when he went to college. He found out they don't allow boa constrictors in the dorms. I was really excited at first. I'm not so sure anymore. That boa just kind of sits around all day long. About the only response I ever get from him is when he flicks his tongue in and out. I have to leave cute little mice for him to eat. They sit there looking terrified. And the boa does have a tendency to hug rather vigorously. I think I'd rather keep the mice and give away the boa. Hey, how would you like a nice boa constrictor?

Did you take a vacation this summer? We went to a dude ranch. I don't think I will be able to sit for another few weeks. Riding horses is not as much fun as I thought it would be. They seem to slobber a lot. My brother was thrown from his horse. It didn't like him. I can understand that.

Write me a letter when you can, Caleb.

Your friend,
Marshall

Choose one assignment from the A section and one from the B section:

A: Write a three-paragraph letter to your best friend about something you did last summer, what you want to do this weekend, what you want to be when you grow up, or anything you want.

Write a two-paragraph letter to a parent stating why you think you should have a raise in your allowance, a telephone in your room, your own room, or anything you would like.

Write a two- or three-paragraph letter to your new pen pal to introduce yourself.

B: Write a two-paragraph letter to a movie studio explaining why they should cast you in their next movie.

Write a three-paragraph letter to the school explaining why school should be held only three days per week.

Write a two-paragraph letter to your teacher explaining why he or she should give you an "A" on your next report card.

The Paragraph Work Sheet

Here is a form to help you plan your paragraph. This will help you narrow down your ideas to a specific topic, and it will also help you choose the supporting points you will want to use in your body sentences.

Step	**Example**
1. Choose a main idea and write it on line 1 below.	*Family*
2. Select a subject from your main idea and write it on line 2.	*My father*
3. Narrow your subject and write it on line 3.	*All the things that my dad does*
4. Brainstorm or cluster for ideas and write them on line 4.	*He works, goes to school, runs marathons, volunteers as a tutor, helps me with my homework, cooks, and plants vegetables*
5. Write the topic sentence on line 5.	*My dad does many things, but the things he does that I like the best are the things that help me the most.*
6. Select ideas to support your topic sentence and write them on line 6.	*helps with homework, cooks, and plants vegetables*

Paragraph Plan

1. _____
2. _____
3. _____
4. _____
5. _____
6. _____

Extension: Now that you have planned a paragraph, write it! Be sure to use the ideas on line 6 to support your topic sentence and to write a concluding sentence as your last sentence.

Check It Off!

Before you turn in your paragraph to your teacher, check to make sure you have made it the best paragraph you can. Check off each item on this list. If you forgot something, it's not too late to go back and catch it.

❏ Prewriting, planning, and organizing have been done.

❏ The paragraph has just one main idea or topic.

❏ Sentences are arranged in an order that makes sense.

❏ Spelling and grammar mistakes have been corrected.

❏ The paragraph has been rewritten to make it better.

❏ The paragraph body has good details, examples, and descriptions.

❏ The sentences are smooth and natural.

❏ A variety of sentences has been used (simple, complex, etc.)

❏ The beginnings of the sentences vary.

❏ Any sentences that do not belong have been taken out, changed, or rearranged.

❏ Transitions have been used.

❏ All sentences are complete thoughts.

❏ All sentences make sense and are connected to the main idea.

❏ Strong, active words are used.

❏ The paragraph is interesting; readers will learn something and/or be entertained.

❏ Writing is fresh and original.

❏ The paragraph has been proofread one last time.

❏ The paragraph is typed or written neatly with the first line indented.

Paragraph Pass

Make one or more copies of pages 37–39. Cut the Paragraph Pass strips from each page. Post the strips throughout the room—on bulletin boards or taped to desktops, for instance. Divide the class into teams of four. Have each team choose a captain. At the signal, the teams walk toward an empty paragraph strip, and work together to complete it. (**Hint:** They may make it a group effort, or they may assign each team member a specific sentence.) When they have finished filling in a paragraph, they need to read it to make sure that it makes sense and that the sentences are complete. When they are sure they have a good paragraph, they sign it with the team captain's last name and look for another paragraph to complete. When all the paragraphs have been filled in, collect them to read aloud to the class. If the paragraph passes (stays on topic, has complete sentences, etc.), the team that wrote it scores one point. The team with the most points wins.

There are several reasons why a person might paint his or her toenails blue.	There are many uses for bubble gum.
One reason is _____ _____ _____ _____	First, _____ _____ _____ _____
Another reason is_____ _____ _____ _____	Another use is _____ _____ _____ _____
A person may also want blue toenails because _____ _____	Bubble gum is also useful for _____ _____ _____ _____
The last reason is _____ _____ _____ _____	Finally, _____ _____ _____ _____

Paragraph Pass *(cont.)*

Homework should be banned.	First of all, _____	Second, _____	Furthermore, _____	Therefore, _____
There are some foods that no one should have to eat, ever.	First, _____	Next, _____	Also, _____	Thus, _____
There are some things that are really scary!	For instance, _____	In addition, _____	Moreover, there is (are) _____	_____ is (are) really scary too!

Paragraph Pass *(cont.)*

Wearing makeup is not such a great idea.	First, _____	Second, _____	Next, _____	Aa a result, _____
Being a mailman is a tough job.	One reason is _____	Another is that _____	And then, _____	Finally, _____
Slipping on a banana peel is funny for several reasons.	First of all, _____	Second, _____	In fact, _____	In short, _____

Party Paragraphs

Cut out the following topic sentences and paste each one on an index card. Pin or tape a card to the back of each student without letting the student see it. Give each student a blank index card. The object of the game is to discover the topic of the paragraph written on one's back and what kind of paragraph it is (descriptive, persuasive, etc.). As the students walk around the room, they read each other's topic sentences and add supporting sentences to each other's blank cards, without stating what the topic is. For instance, if the topic is "Peanut butter is gooey and good," the supporting sentences will not mention the words "peanut butter." All sentences should also support the type of paragraph specified. Students may add supporting sentences until the card is full, using both sides of the index card, if necessary. To determine their own topics, the players must pay close attention to the content and nature of the sentences written on their index cards

Here is the best way to make a pizza. (*Expository*)	The rules of football are not that difficult to understand. (*Expository*)
Our classroom is an interesting place. (*Descriptive*)	A tree is a beautiful thing. (*Descriptive*)
Children in America are really different from children in China. (*Contrast*)	Boys and girls like different things. (*Contrast*)
Our class should take a field trip to Disneyland. (*Persuasive*)	Brown is an ugly color. (*Opinion*)
Here is a typical day in our classroom. (*Narrative*)	There are many things to do when camping. (*Narrative*)
If you want to learn to skateboard, here is how to start. (*Expository*)	A big motorcycle is an awesome sight. (*Descriptive*)
Our school is like many other schools in our state. (*Comparison*)	Hamburgers and hot dogs are similar foods. (*Compare*)
We should not have homework. (*Persuasive*)	We should be able to stay up as late as we want. (*Persuasive*)
Summer is an interesting time of the year. (*Definitive*)	Boys and girls should go to separate schools. (*Opinion*)
Planting a garden is fun. (*Narrative*)	A banana is a strange food. (*Definitive*)

Scrambled Paragraphs

Copy the paragraphs below, or create your own paragraphs. Cut the sentences apart (paragraphs can be mounted and laminated before being cut, if you wish). Be sure to make at least one set of uncut copies so that the students can use a copy to check their own.

For each student, mix together all of the sentences. Let the students unscramble them to make eight paragraphs. Students who complete all eight first win a prize (stickers, pencils, go-to-lunch-first passes, etc.). To make the game a little less challenging, scramble together the sentences of only two to four paragraphs at a time.

I don't like to go shopping. First of all, it takes time to get to the mall. Then it takes even more time to walk around looking for things. Lots of times it takes a long time to find things, and then, sometimes there is a wait at the dressing rooms. When I try things on, they often don't fit or look funny on me. Usually I go home with nothing at all! Shopping is a big pain.

Jeremy Lundbuster loves to eat. For breakfast he will eat four eggs, four pieces of toast with butter and jam, a bowl of cereal, and a cinnamon roll. At school he eats his lunch in the classroom at 10 A.M. and calls his mom to bring him another lunch. At lunchtime he is not finished eating when the bell rings, so he finishes and then goes to class. After school he has cookies, corn on the cob, pizza, and artichokes. He eats all of his dinner and asks for seconds before he starts on dessert. He even has a bedtime snack. And the strangest thing of all is that he is as skinny as a broomstick!

I love music. I like to play it in my room and turn the volume up. I like to dance to it. I like to sing along and pretend that I am a rock star. Music makes me feel good. I love music.

Scrambled Paragraphs *(cont.)*

Green is the color of nature. Everywhere we look we see this color. It's in the trees, the grass, the leaves, and the plants. It's the color of all living plants. Chlorophyll makes plants green. Green plants are healthy for humans, animals, and insects to eat. Green is everywhere.

I like to go camping. First of all, I can get dirty and not shower, and no one cares. I like to sleep outside and watch for shooting stars. I get to see lots of animals like deer, raccoons, and even bears. Food tastes better when it has been cooked over a campfire. Roasted marshmallows and s'mores are the best. I can get wild and crazy out in the woods, and it's okay. Camping is a lot of fun.

Leticia Morganstar likes to draw. When she was a baby, she drew a portrait of her parents on the wall with peanut butter. When she was older, she drew a mural of the American Revolution on her bedroom wall. In school she drew on her spelling tests and had to stay after class. She drew caterpillars on her sneakers, unicorns on her lunchbox, and bicycles on her eraser. One day Leticia Morganstar will be a famous artist; I just know it!

We should always have four-day weekends. Two days are not enough. If we had four days, we would have time to go visit our grandparents and other relatives. We might also have time to go and see some interesting places like battlefields, museums, or art galleries and do lots of educational things. If we had four days we would have time to clean up our rooms and finish our homework. We'd also have more time to rest and have some fun. I say we should all take four-day weekends from now on!

I don't like homework. I'd rather be watching TV than doing homework. I'd also rather be talking to my friends on the telephone or playing games with my little brother. My mom says I have to do it. My teachers say I have to do it. I don't know why I have to do it, but I know that everyone is unhappy if I don't do it. And I am the only one who is unhappy if I do it. I guess that is just the way things are.

Paragraph Matching

Cut out the Topic Sentences and Body Sentences cards. Pass out all of the cards so that each student has either a Topic Sentences or Body Sentences card. At your signal, the students walk about the room reading their cards aloud repeatedly. They are to speak in a normal tone and not shout. When a student finds his or her match (the topic sentence and body sentences fit), the pair goes to a designated place in the classroom where they line up in order. Give rewards to those who finish first. To play for points, create many more cards and play for an extended amount of time.

Topic Sentences

My cousin Michael is a nut.	I wish I could eat all I want.
I hate to rollerskate!	I'd like a pet opossum.
Weddings always make me cry.	Television is stupid.
I could live on chocolate chip cookies.	I wish I were a movie star.
I would like to stay up all night.	I'd like to be seven feet tall.

Paragraph Matching *(cont.)*

Body Sentences

First of all, he is always laughing at things. Everything is funny to him. Another thing is that he goes through his family's mail and reads it all aloud. He also asks really strange questions like, "Why is your hair that color?" He is as nutty as can be.	I am always falling down and hurting myself. When I am not falling down, I look really silly trying to keep my balance. I can't seem to move unless I am holding unto something and pulling myself along. I will never do it again!
Food is so great! There is crunchy food, spicy food, sweet food, and yummy food. There is smooth food and hot and cold food. Eating is fun and delicious. If I could, I would eat as much as I want, but I get full. If I eat too much, I get a stomachache, and that's no fun. Then I have to stop eating and not eat again until I am hungry. It's not fair!	I have so many things to do and not enough time to do them all. I could just keep reading, or drawing, or talking to my friends. It gets really quiet at night, and I can think and talk to myself then. I could get all caught up with my homework and read all my favorite books. I could even raid the refrigerator. I wish I didn't have to go to sleep each night.
I would be able to reach all the highest shelves in the library. I would also be able to find my friends in any crowd. My shoes would be really big. Best of all, the best teams would want me to play basketball for them.	First of all, they are so funny looking. If I could walk down the street with one on a leash, everyone would stare. Next, they are good at climbing and hiding. I could play hide and seek with my pet. They mostly eat fruits and vegetables, so I could give them some of my food. And what's really cool is when they pretend that they are dead.
I don't know why it is. It may be the music or the flowers or all the love in the air. It may be because I see the mother of the bride with her mascara running down her face. I'm not sure what it is, but I need to always remember to take a hankie to weddings.	Sure, it was a great invention, but there are too many stupid things being broadcast. My brothers and sisters watch some cartoons that make very little sense. There are lots of silly car chases, movie star news shows, and soap operas. There are even people selling silly exercise machines, dolls, jewelry, and tapes of the Monkees. There is a lot of silly and stupid stuff on television.
First of all, they are delicious. Second of all, they are easy to make, and they can be bought anywhere. They also give me energy and make me feel good. I never get tired of eating them.	Everybody would want my autograph. I'd get paid lots of money just for being in a movie. I would be able to travel all over the world. I'd be interviewed on television. It would be great!

Paragraph Matching (cont.)

More Topic Sentences	**More Body Sentences**
Ice cream is not that enjoyable to eat.	First, it melts faster than I can eat it, and it drips on my shoes. It makes everything sticky: my mouth, my fingers, and the floor. It's almost too sweet sometimes, and some flavors, like "honey-roasted pistachio," are a little strange. I guess it's okay, but it's not as great as everyone says.
Gifts are the best fun of all!	I love to get them, most of all. They are all wrapped up in colorful paper, and my imagination goes crazy wondering what is inside. They are fun to open. The best way is to just tear into the paper. They are fun to give, too. It's fun to watch a person who is surprised by an unexpected gift.
Kittens may be cute, but they give me the creeps.	First of all, they may be really cute, but they are so unpredictable. They will jump out at me from under the furniture and attack my feet with all their claws. They hiss and pretend that they are ferocious lions. They climb up the curtains or window screens, and you don't notice them until you walk by. That is very scary! They are cute, but they are creepy.
I would like to learn to fly a plane.	What could be better than soaring over the rooftops? I could get to places a lot faster than I would by riding my bike or driving a car. It would be so much fun. I hope I can do it.
I want to be a newspaper reporter when I grow up.	First, they get to go lots of interesting places to cover the news. Next, they get to have their names in the newspapers all the time, and their pictures, too, sometimes. They get to dig up the facts about things and know about what is happening before anyone else does. I just think it would be the most exciting job.

Team Paragraphs

Divide the class into teams of five. Give each team captain one of the topic sentence strips below. If you have more time, give a topic sentence strip to each student and have the teams rotate the position of team captain. At your signal, each team captain goes to the board to write the topic sentence. When the captain has finished, he or she hands the chalk to the next team member who must write the first body sentence to support the topic sentence. The third team member writes the second body sentence, the fourth team member writes the third sentence, and the fifth team member writes a conclusion.

As the paragraphs are completed, number them, giving a #1 to the first-place finisher, #2 for the second-place finisher, and so on. When there is a paragraph on the board for each team, pause to read the paragraphs. The prizes (stickers, computer time, etc.) go to the team with the first paragraph completed with the least number of errors. Also, be sure that the paragraphs make sense and that the sentences do what they are supposed to be doing, either supporting or closing. If there is time, continue to play.

Everyone should have a basketball hoop.
Tornadoes are amazing.
I like to look at the sky.
There are good things on television.
We should read as much as we can.
Everyone should play a sport.
Babysitting is a difficult job.
We should all ride bikes most places.
Our class should go to Hawaii.
Everyone should learn how to fish.
Toes are funny.
Our school should get a trampoline.
I love rice and beans.
I love to be with my family.
Lizards make great pets.

Team Paragraphs *(cont.)*

It's fun to eat with my hands.
Everyone should get up to see the sun rise.
It's important to play as hard as we work.
Teen magazines are not worth it.
I love to sleep in.
Dogs are better than cats.
Dancing is fun.
Baseball is boring.
I like rainy days.
I don't like tapioca pudding.
Everyone should have a computer.
There are many uses for pine cones.
Left-handed people are different.
We should laugh at something everyday.
Many people are driving too fast.
We should be able to take our pets to school.
I love bread!
Licorice is a disgusting taste.
We should have electric cars.
Being sick has some advantages and disadvantages.
I love chocolate!

Answer Key

Page 8

Answers will vary. Here are some possibilities.

2. We would all benefit from sports. Sports are good for us.

3. I think cars should be made of rubber. It would be better if cars were made of rubber.

4. I love pizza! Pizza is good for us.

5. Amusement parks are fun. I like amusement parks.

6. I deserve to have my own telephone. I need a telephone in my room.

7. There are many things we couldn't do without elbows. Elbows are useful.

8. I like dogs. Dogs are the best pets to have.

Page 9

The following sentences should be crossed out.

1. My sister wants to be a teacher. I don't think that would be as much fun.

2. Skiing is also good to do. Skateboarding is another way to stay in shape when there is no snow.

3. Test taking is easy once you figure out the secrets. Some teachers like to surprise students with a quiz, and some let students know when to study.

4. Professional athletes make lots of money. A manufacturer may sponsor those who get really good at a sport.

5. There are many strange people in the world. I'm not sure whether there are more strange adults or more strange teenagers in the world.

Pages 11–12

Topic sentences will vary.

Page 13

Body sentences will vary.

Page 14

Supporting reasons and sentences will vary.

Page 15

Body sentences will vary, but there need to be connections between the topics and concluding sentences.

Page 16

1. *Grade:* B or C *Comment:* Needs to stay focused a bit more on topic sentence and needs a concluding sentence.

2. *Grade:* B or C *Comment:* The topic sentence is vague. The student probably should have talked about just one of his pets.

3. *Grade:* B or C *Comment:* Topic sentence has too many details which should have been saved for the body sentences. "Best friend's cat" is off the topic, for example.

4. *Grade:* A *Comment:* The topic sentence tells what the paragraph is about. The body sentences support that George is a special rabbit. The concluding sentence summarizes the topic well.

Page 17

(**Note:** This is the original paragraph, but some variations are possible. Check students' responses for chronological sense, even if they vary somewhat from this one.)

I had a very bad day today. First of all, my alarm never went off. I accidentally set it for 6 P.M. instead of 6 A.M. I didn't have time to eat breakfast, so I stopped at the donut store on the way to school. I thought I could get a bagel and some orange juice. They were out of bagels, so I had to get a jelly donut. They were out of orange juice, so I had to get hot chocolate. I ate while I walked to school. Of course, the next thing that happened is the jelly donut spurted and got red stuff down the front of my light blue shirt. When I went to open the hot chocolate, it wouldn't open. Then when I tried really hard, it came open and some of it spilled on my pants! Then it was really hot and burned my tongue. When I got to history the teacher asked for our reports. I thought they were due tomorrow! After school, in track, my pants ripped. I was so embarrassed. When I got home, no one was there, and I had forgotten my keys. When my mom came home, she found me sitting on the front porch. She asked me, "How was your day?" I said, "Don't ask."

Page 18

Transitional phrases will vary. Here are some examples:

1. We're going to have an exchange student next month. First, she needs to send in her papers to the exchange program. Next, she will write us and send her picture. After that, we will write her and send pictures. Finally, she will travel to our country and we will meet her!

2. It's a good idea to get enough rest each night. However, sleeping in too long on the weekends could cause problems. First, it can confuse our bodies, and then we will have trouble sleeping at night. In addition, if we get too much sleep, we waste time and may be too wound up to be able to concentrate. And then, when Monday morning comes, we will be even more tired. So, while it is a good idea to get enough rest, we need to do so in moderation.

3. I was not able to do my homework last night. First of all, my brother broke his arm, and we had to take him to the doctor's office. Then, it was really late when we got home. Nevertheless, I set my alarm to get up early to do my homework. However, I was so tired that I slept through it and had to hurry to get to school!

Page 19

The sentences and conclusions will vary, but they should all make sense and be connected to the topic.